In The Sea

GRAYSCALE PHOTO COLORING BOOK FOR ADULTS

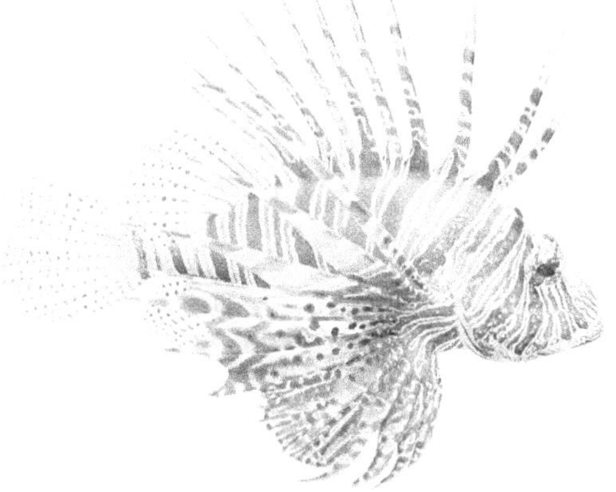

Majestic COLORING

www.MajesticColoring.com

ISBN: 978-1532938252

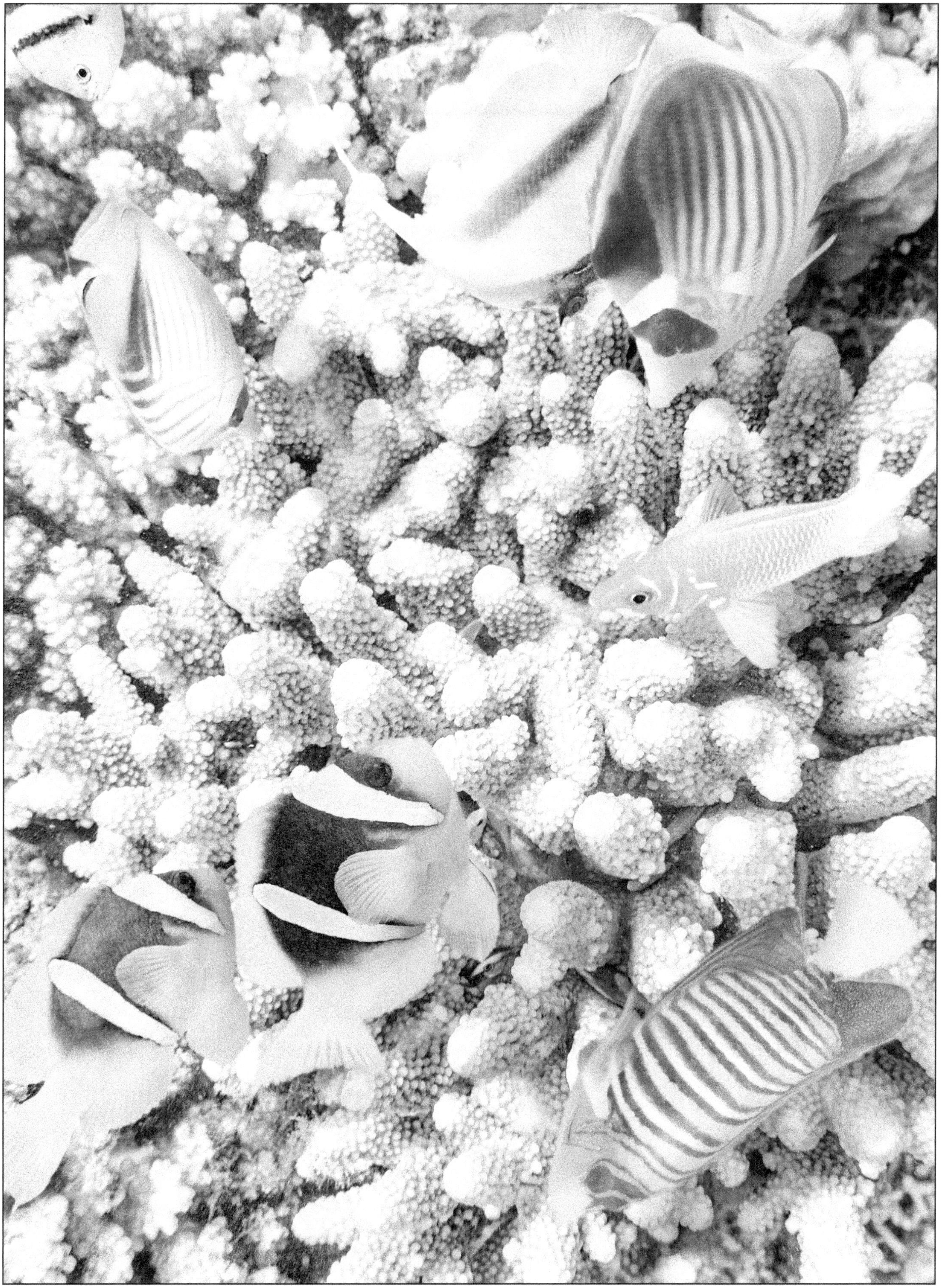

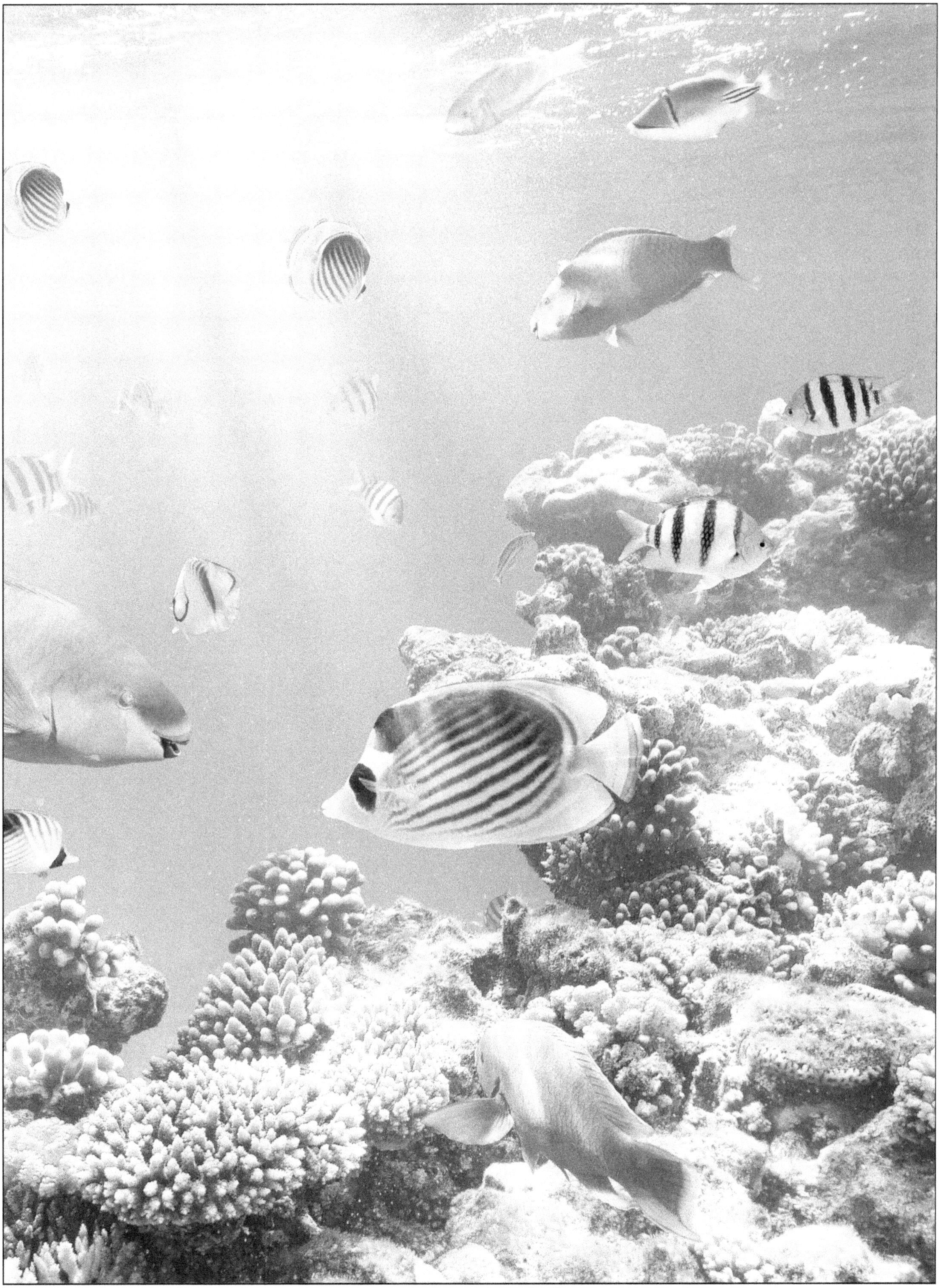

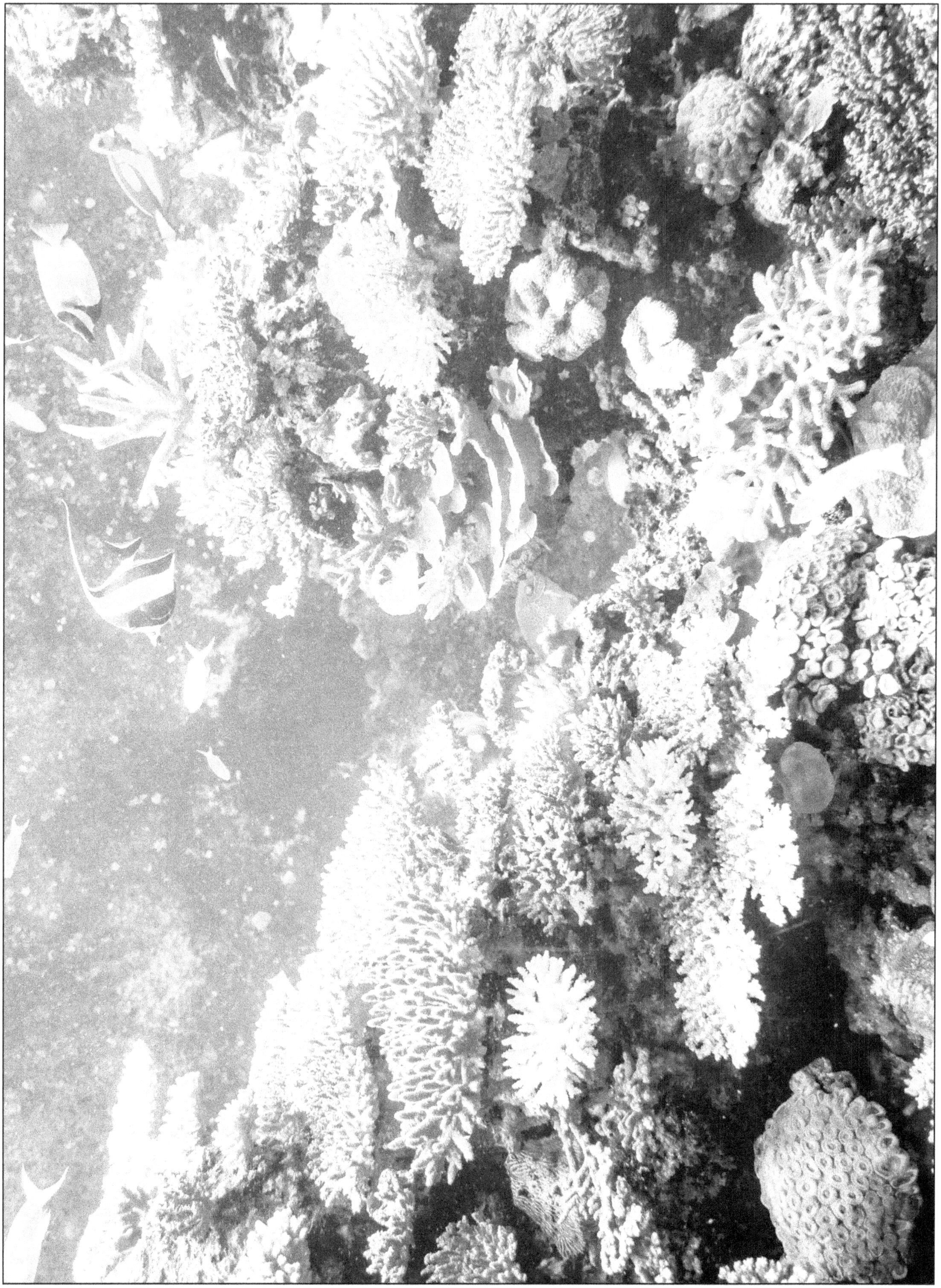

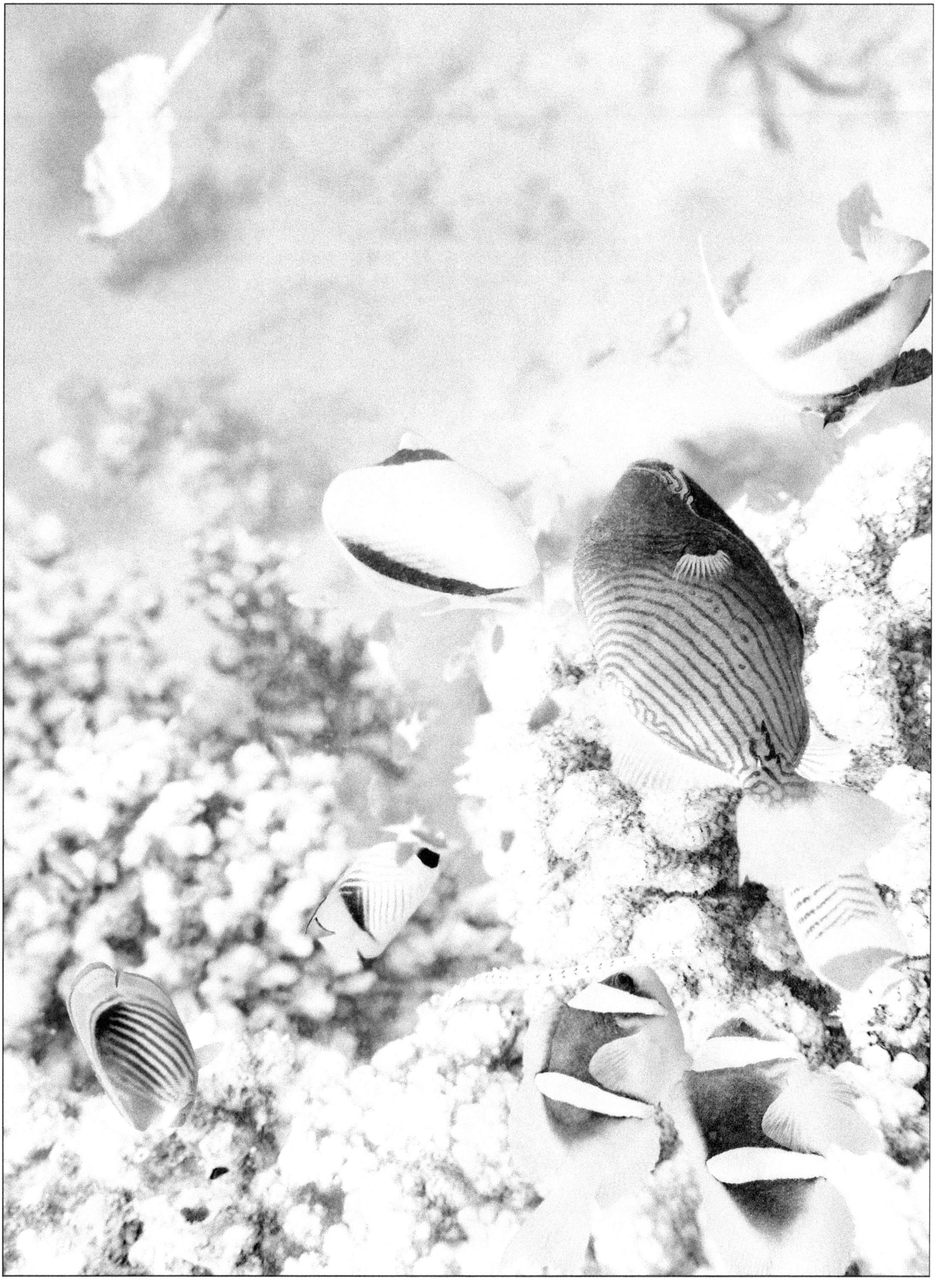

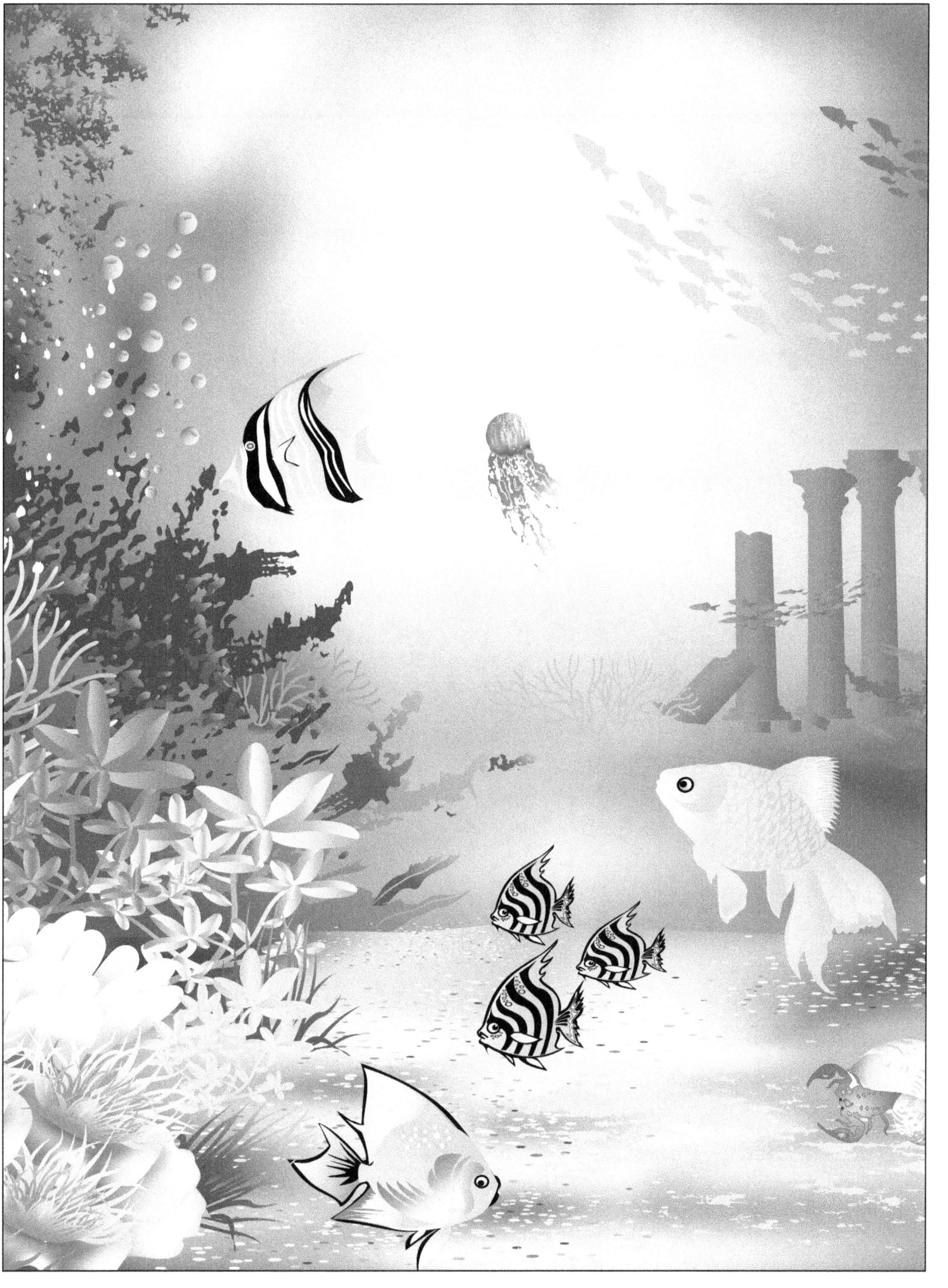

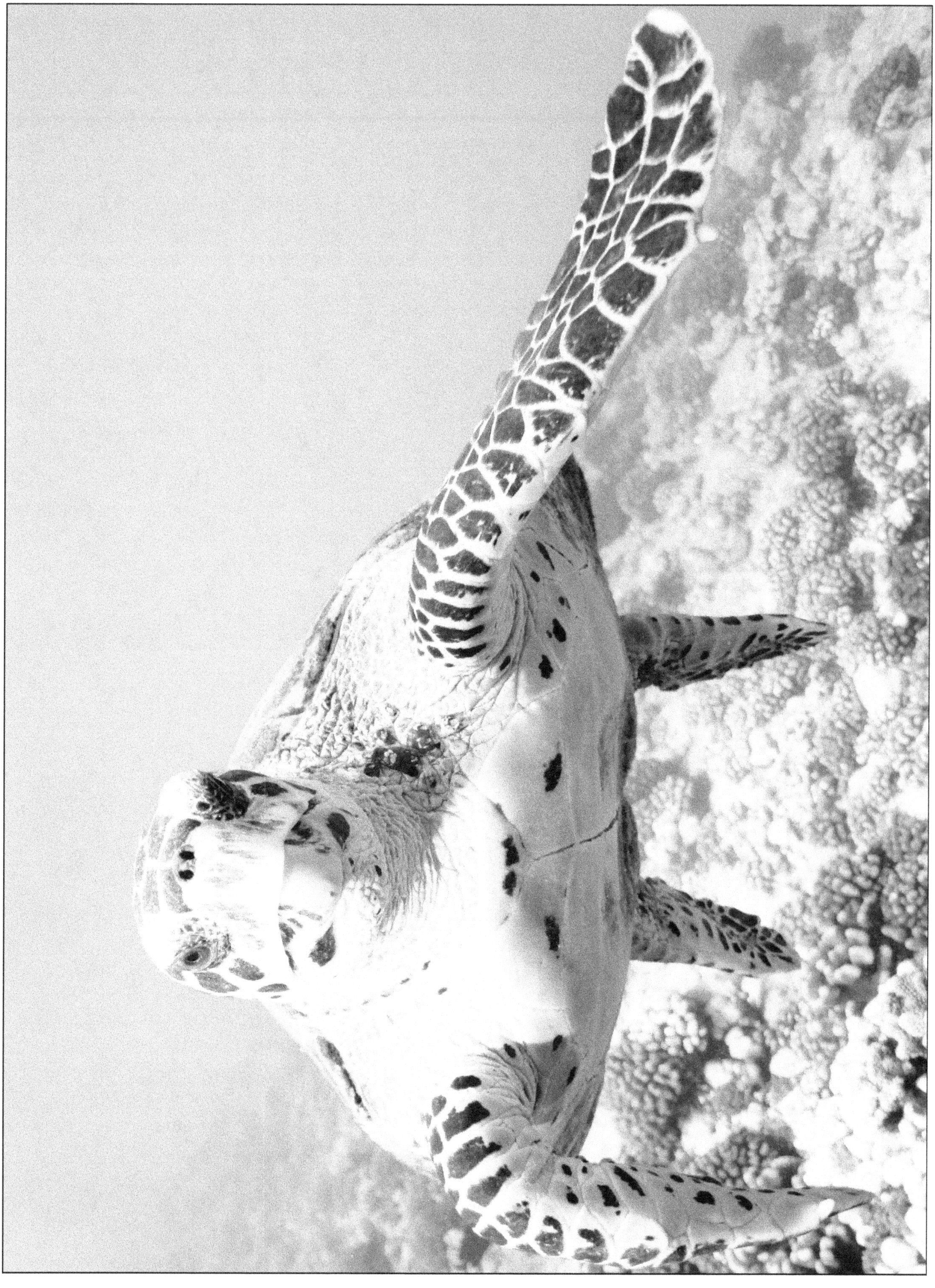

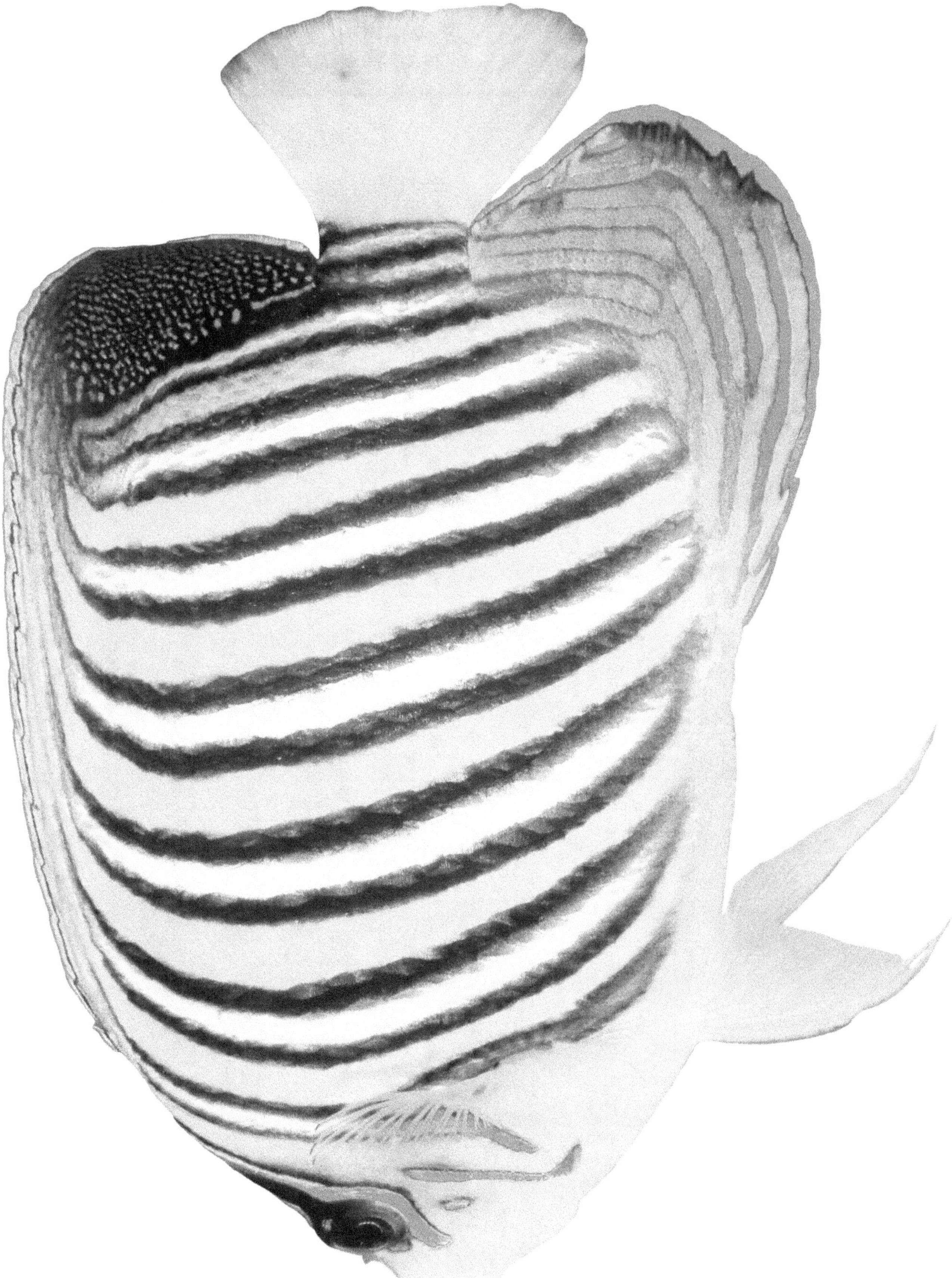

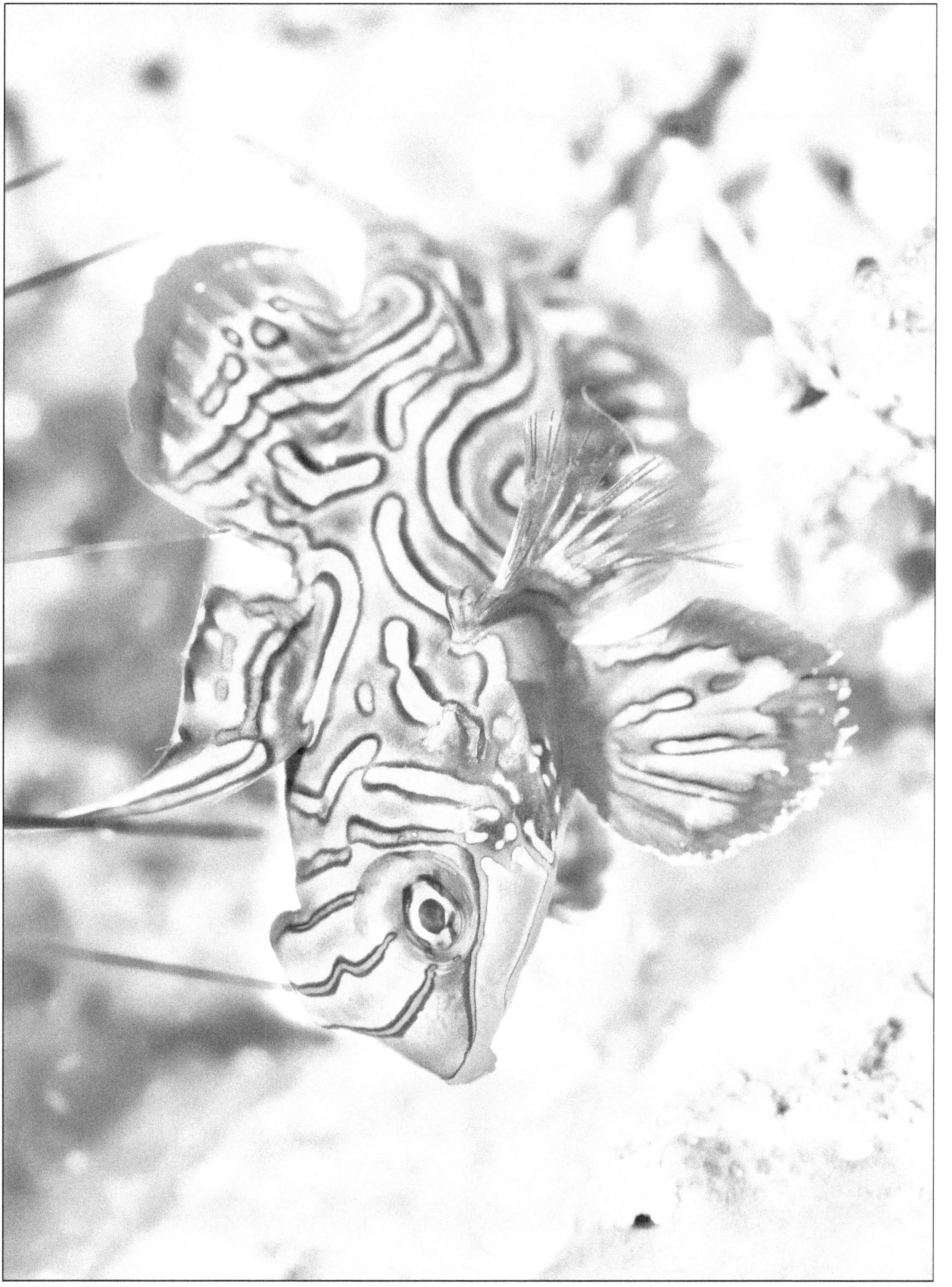

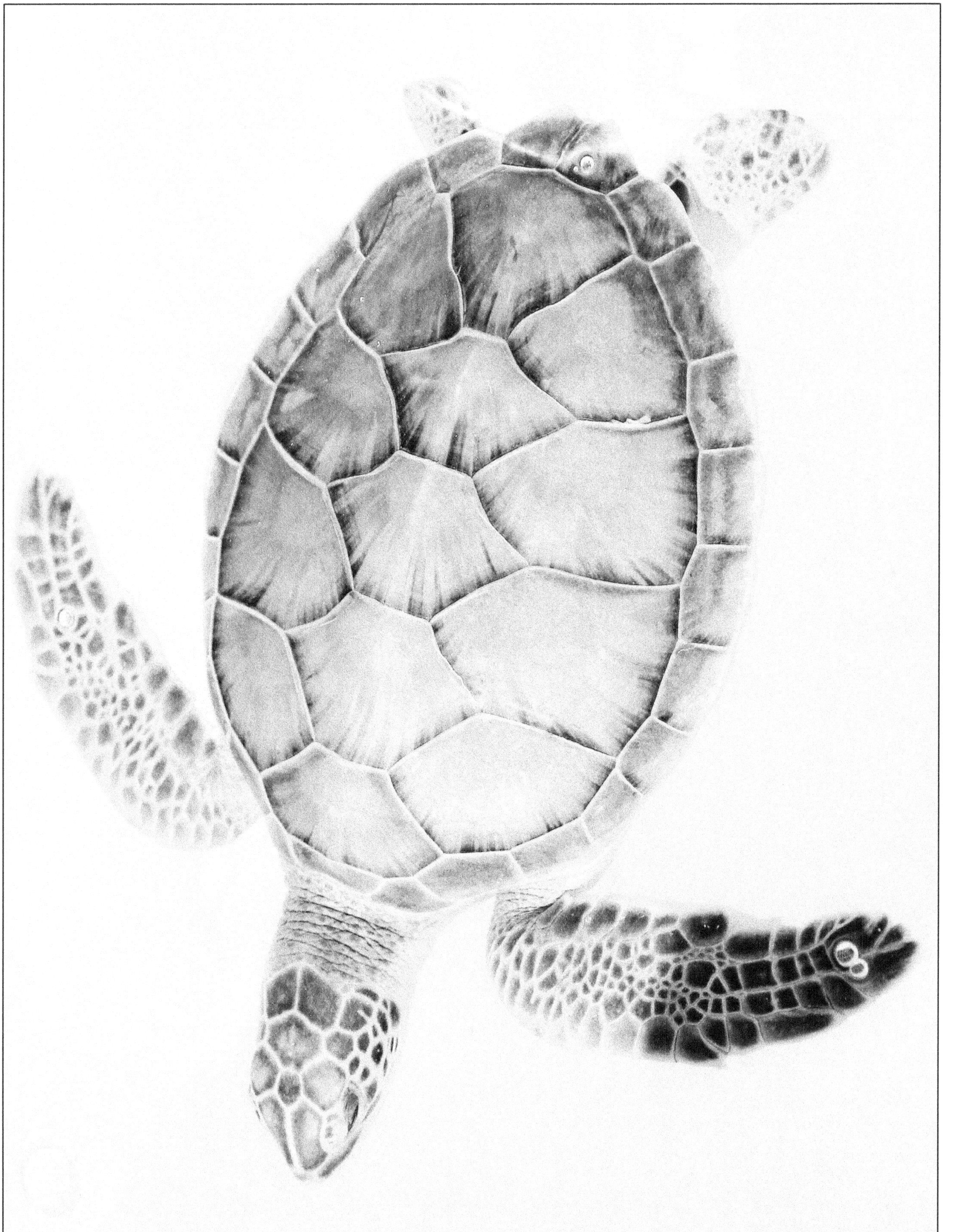

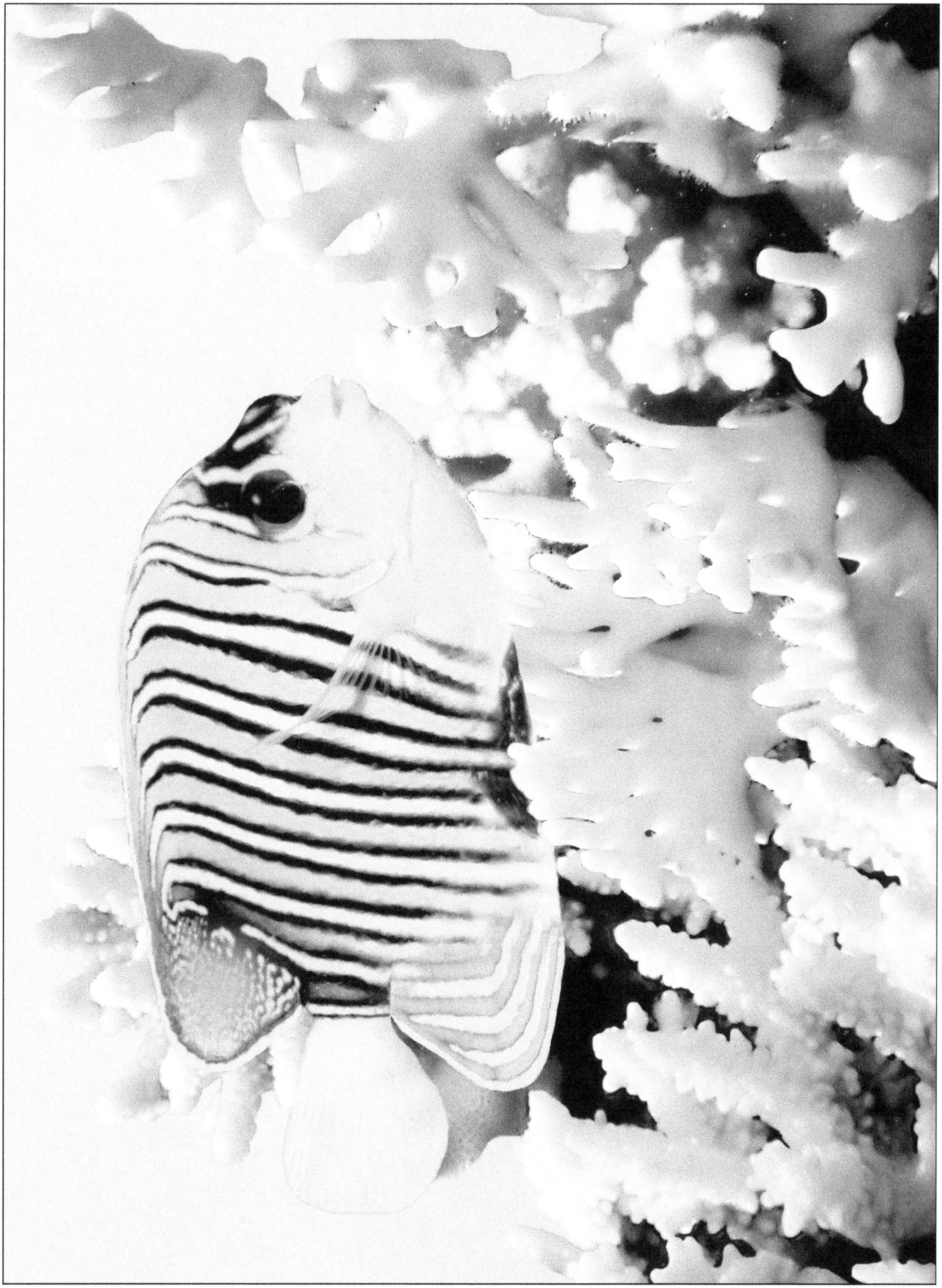

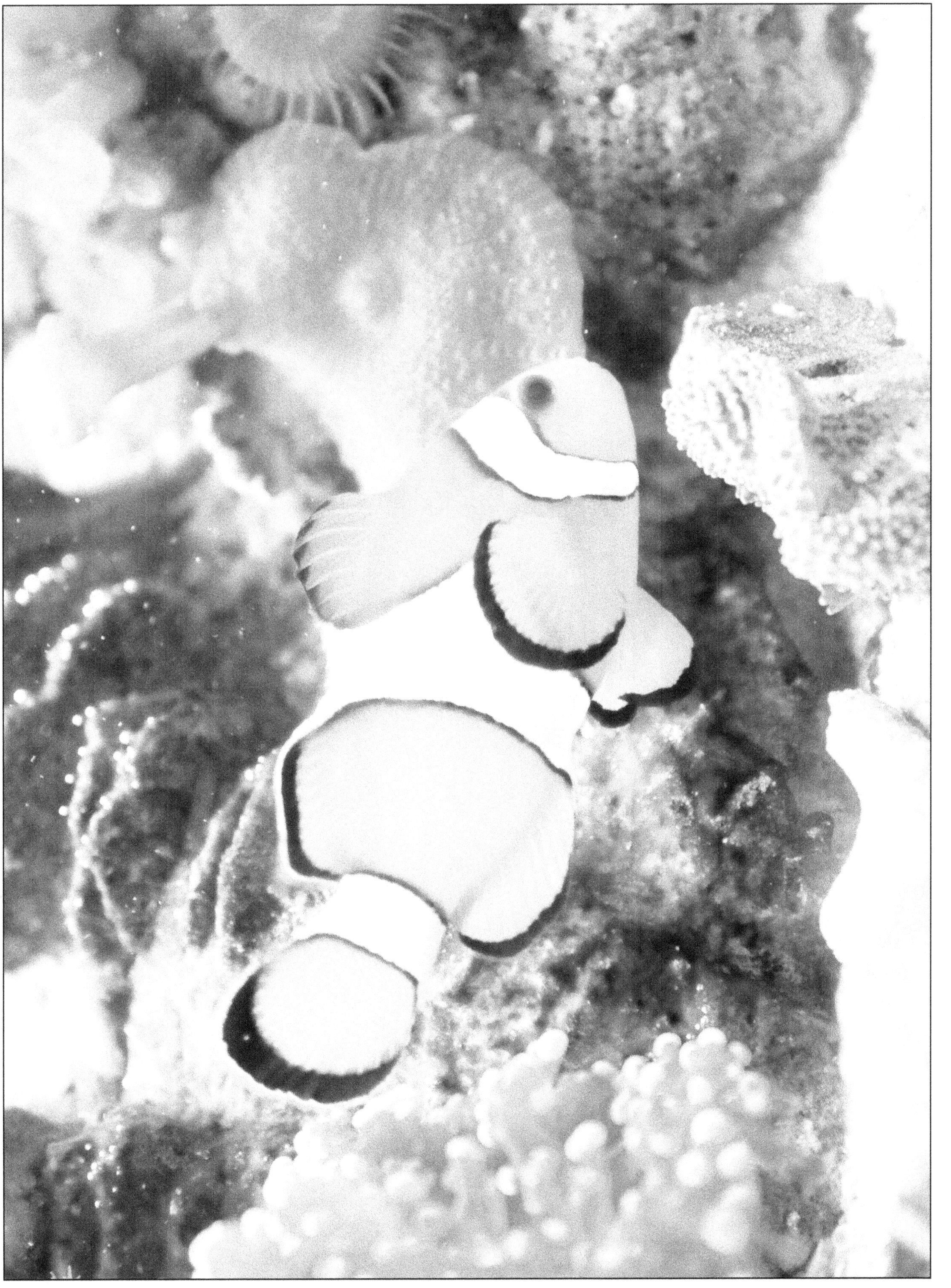

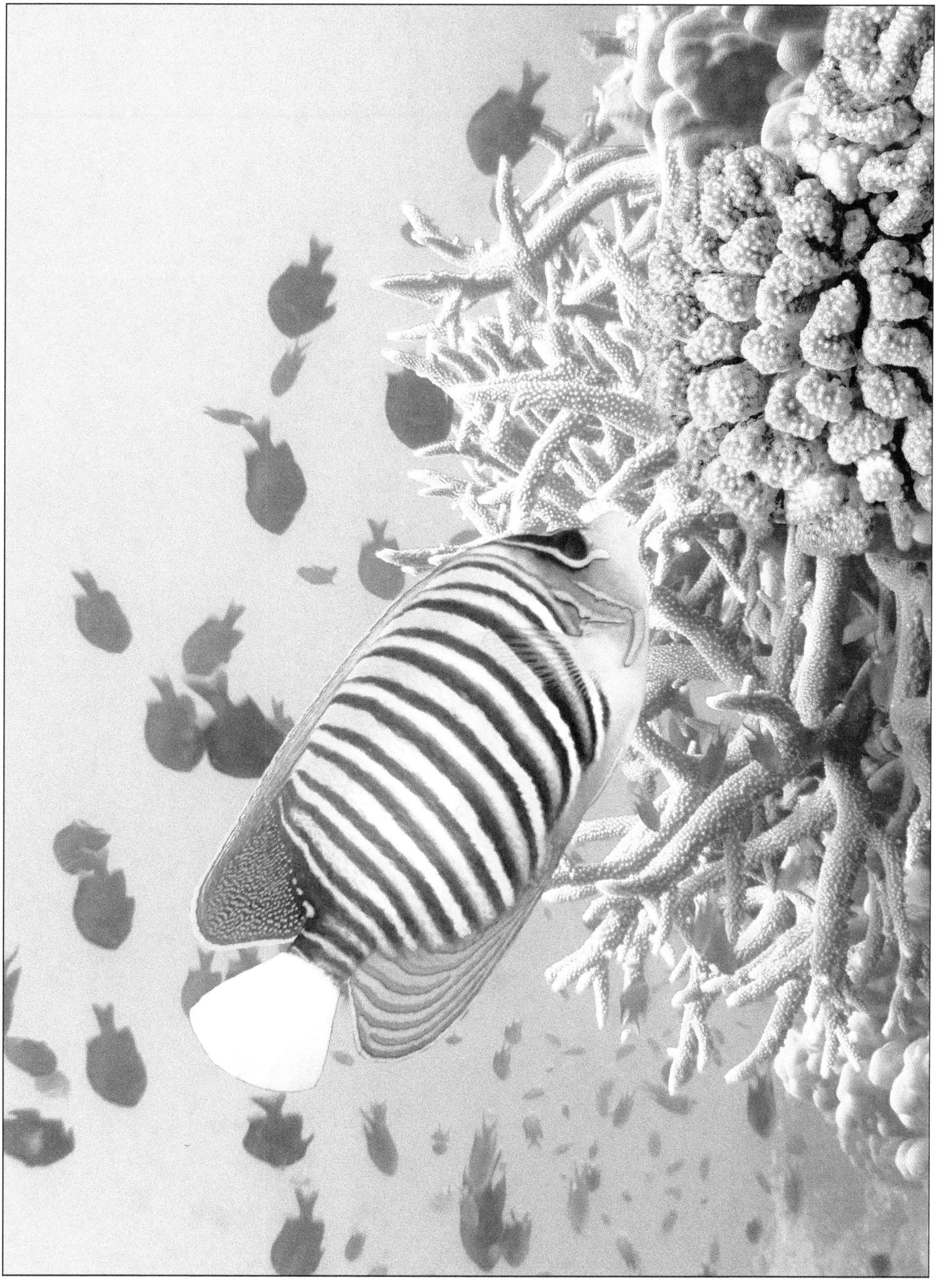

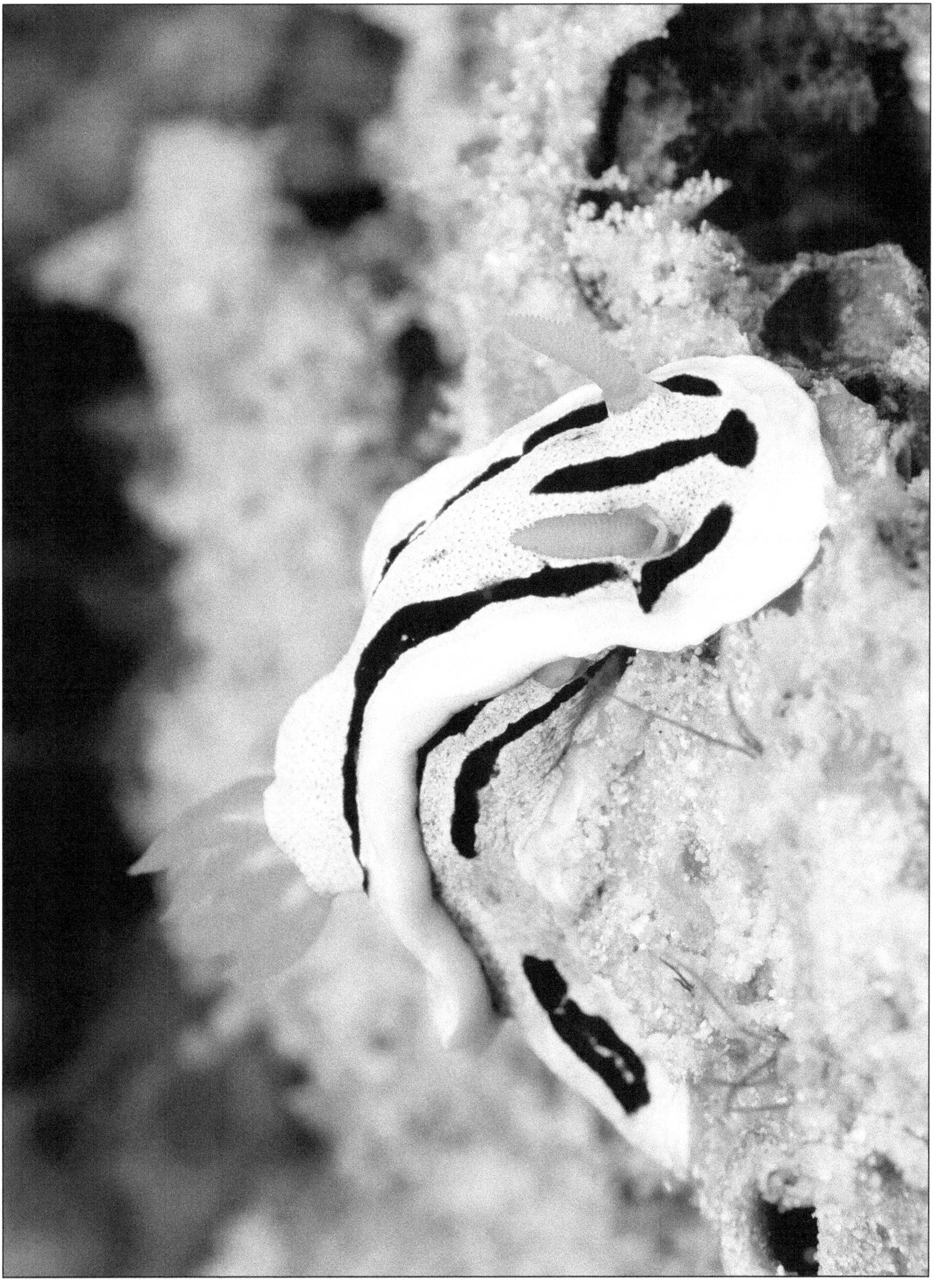

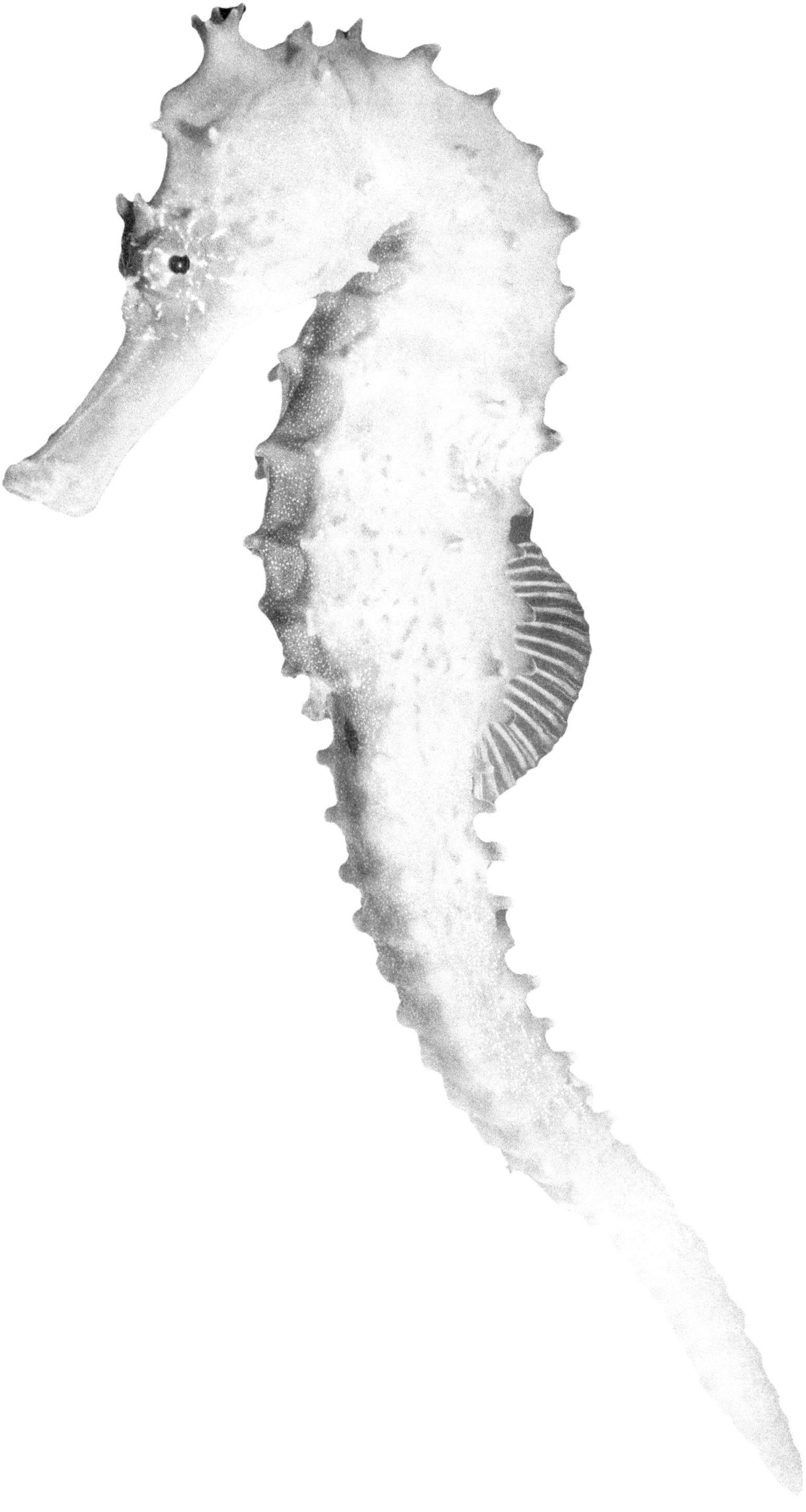

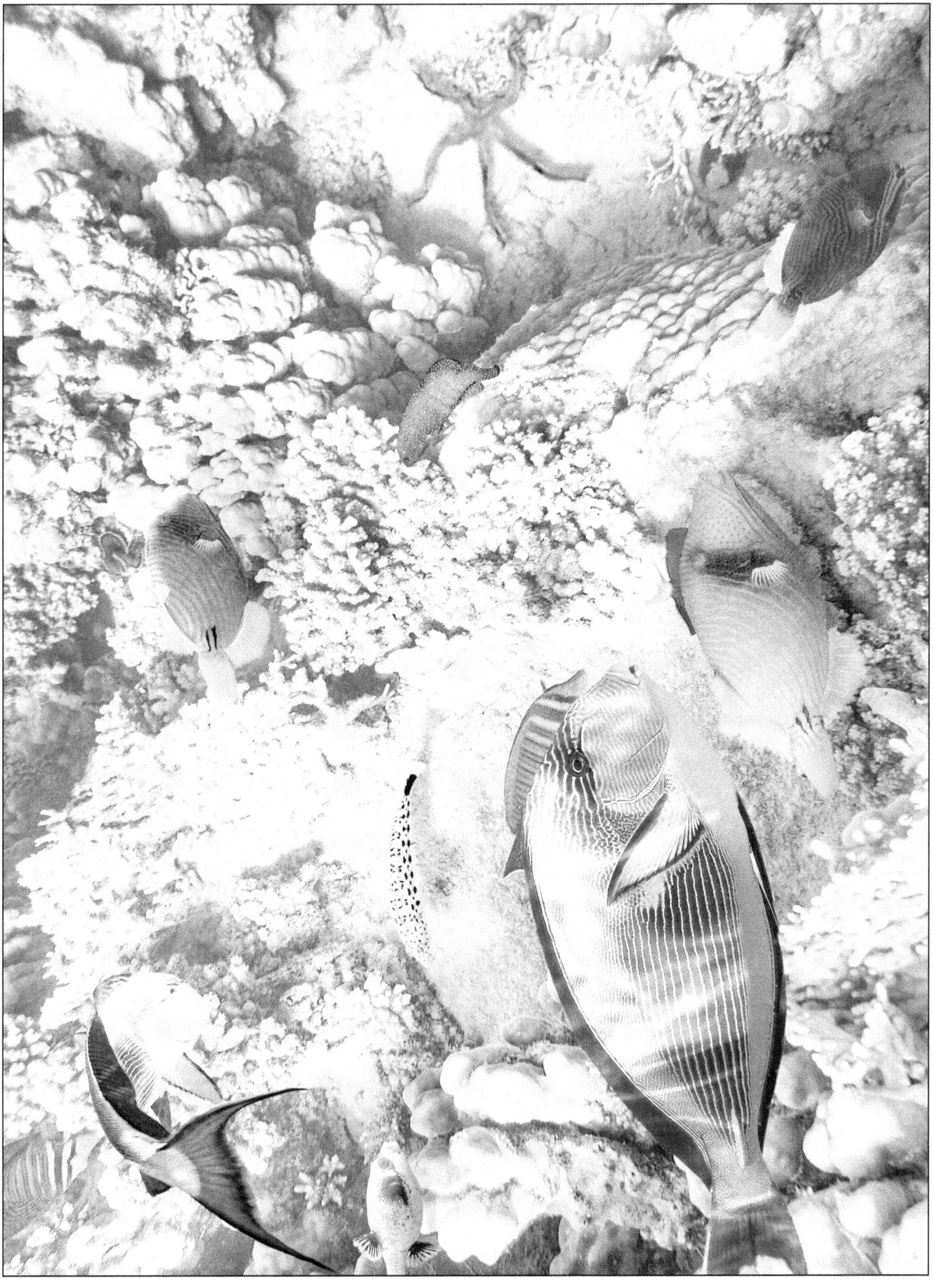

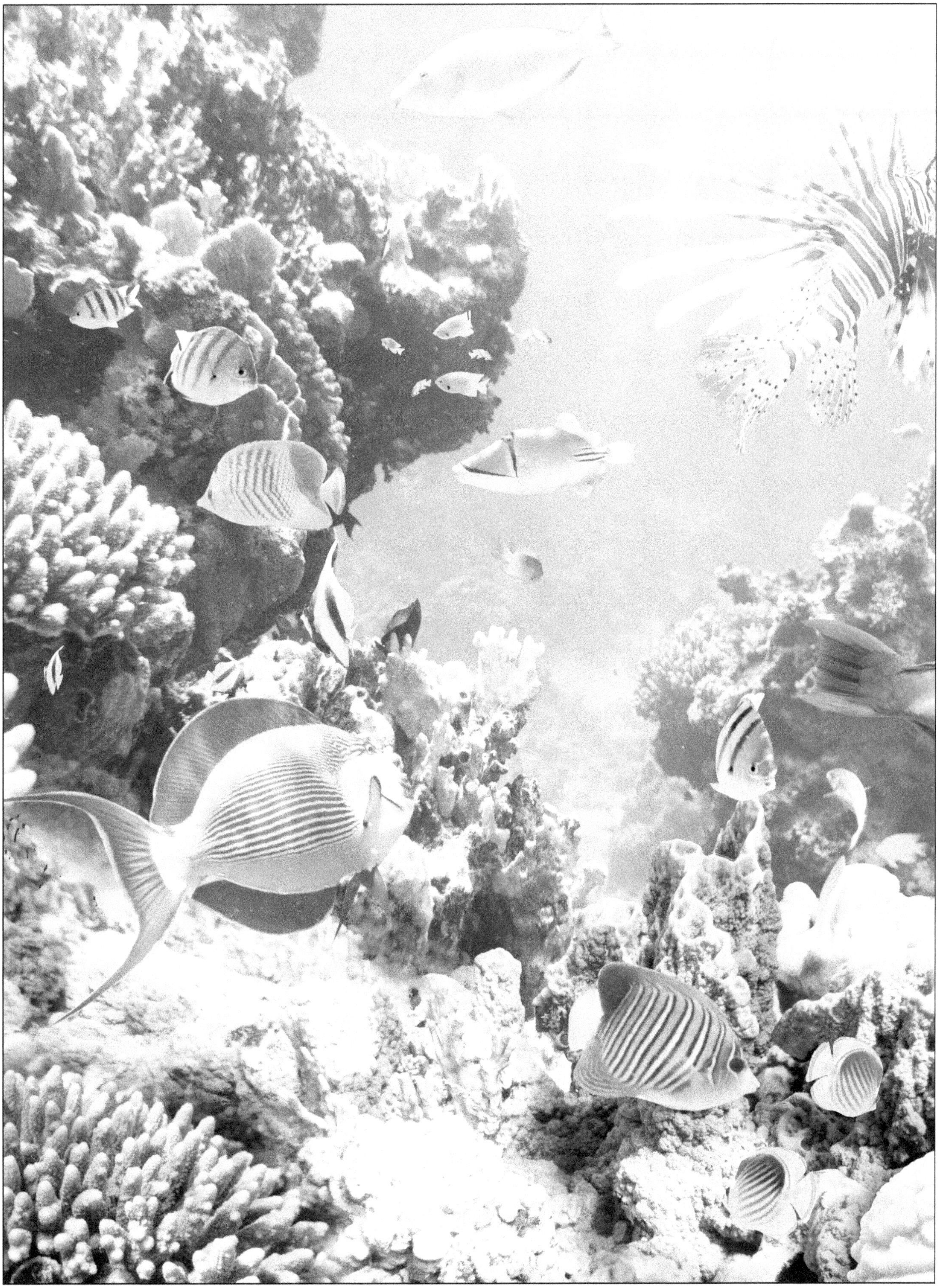

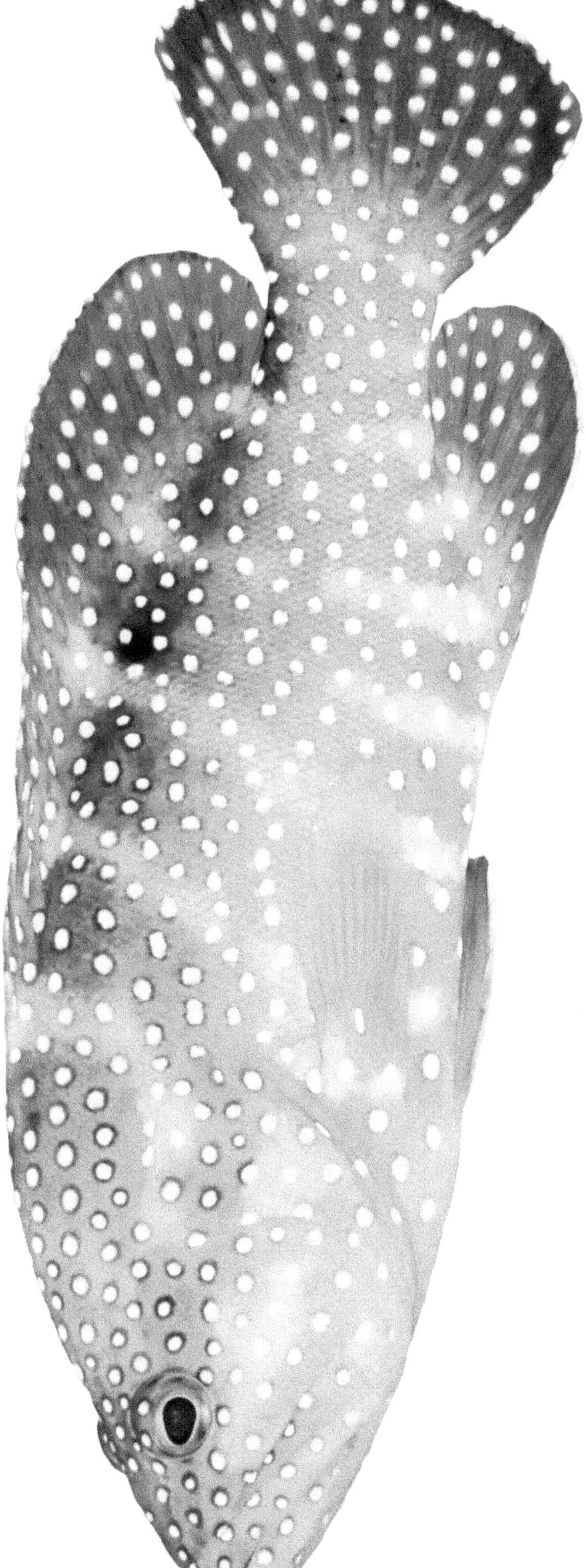

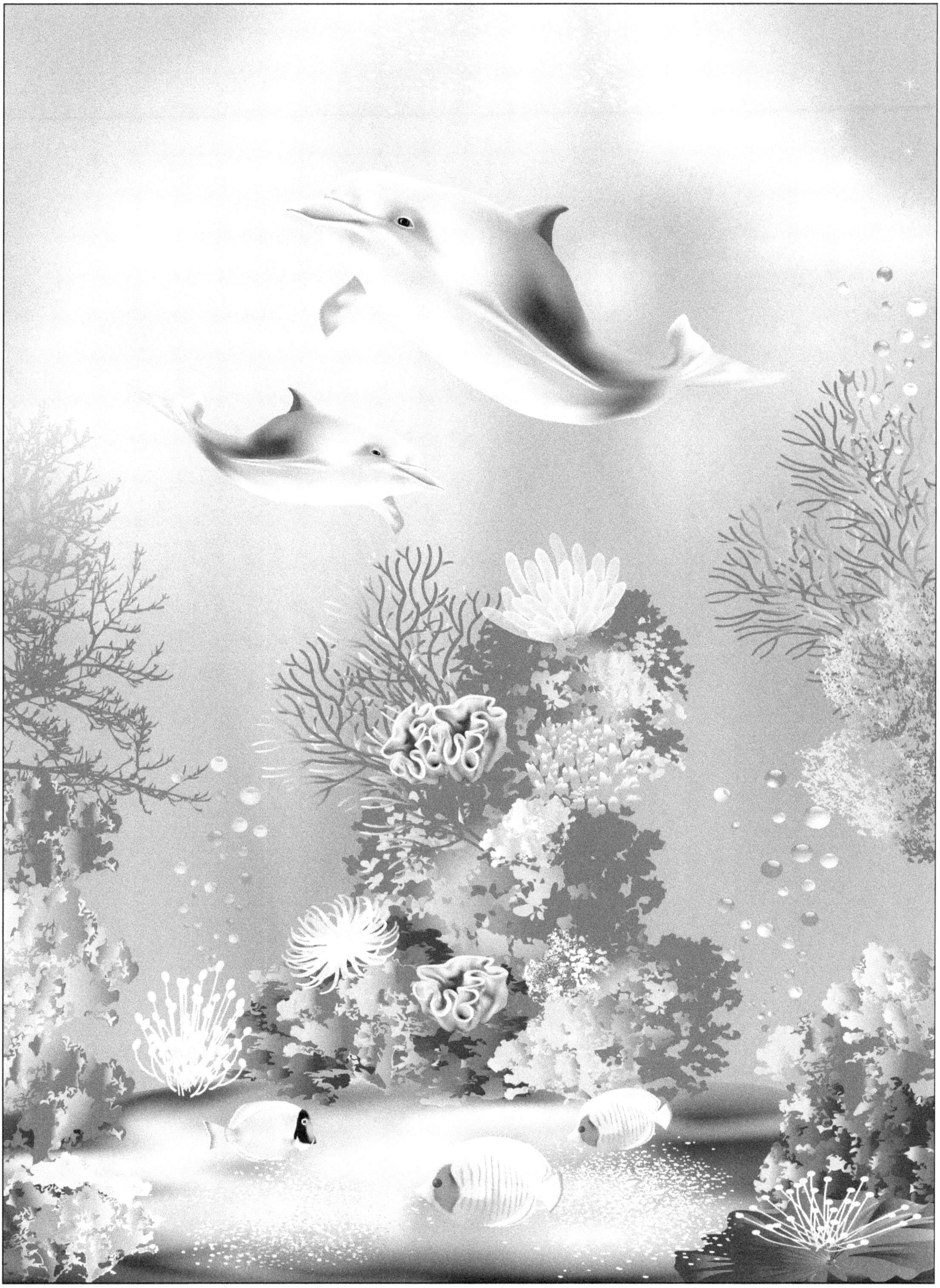

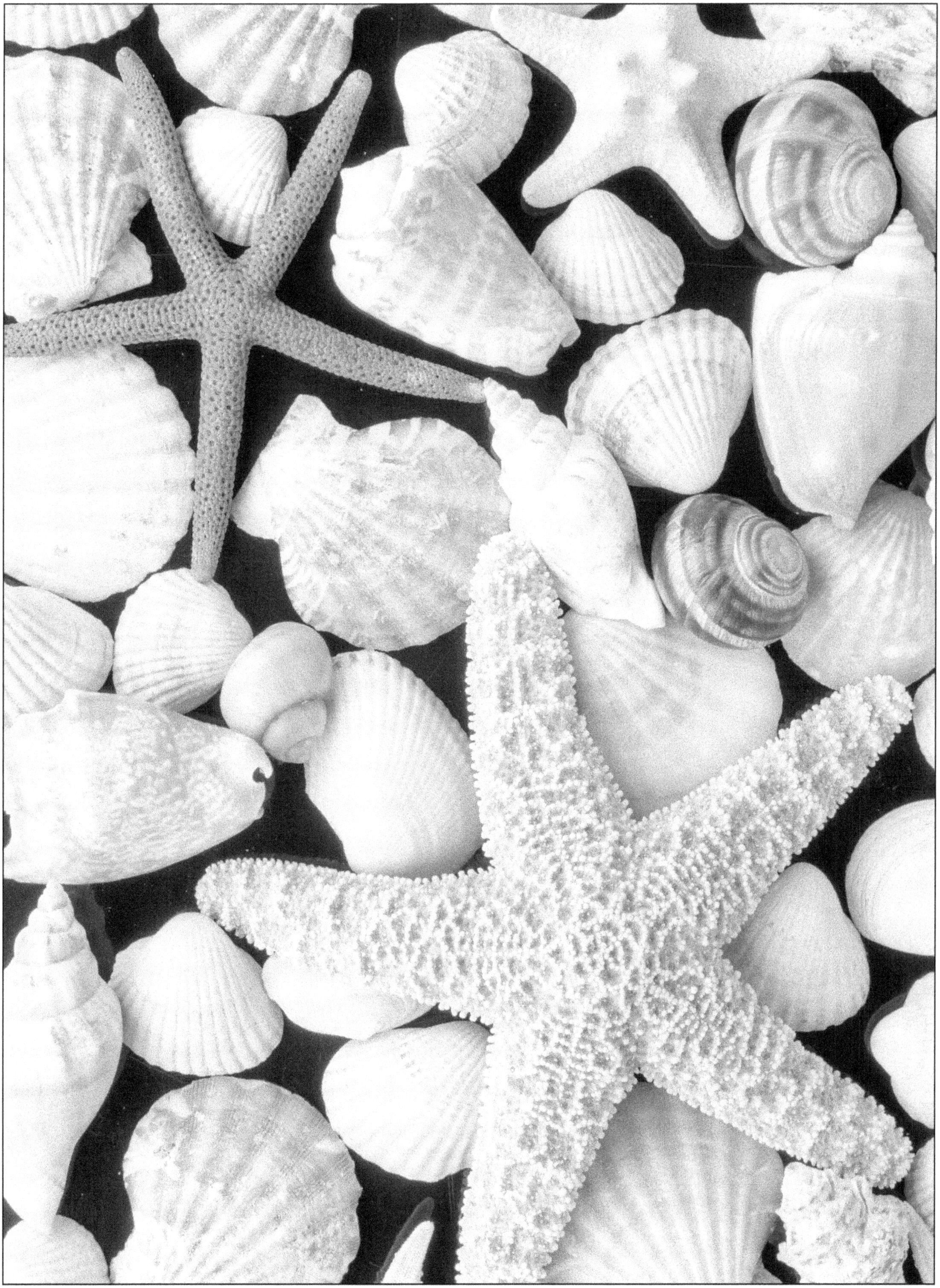

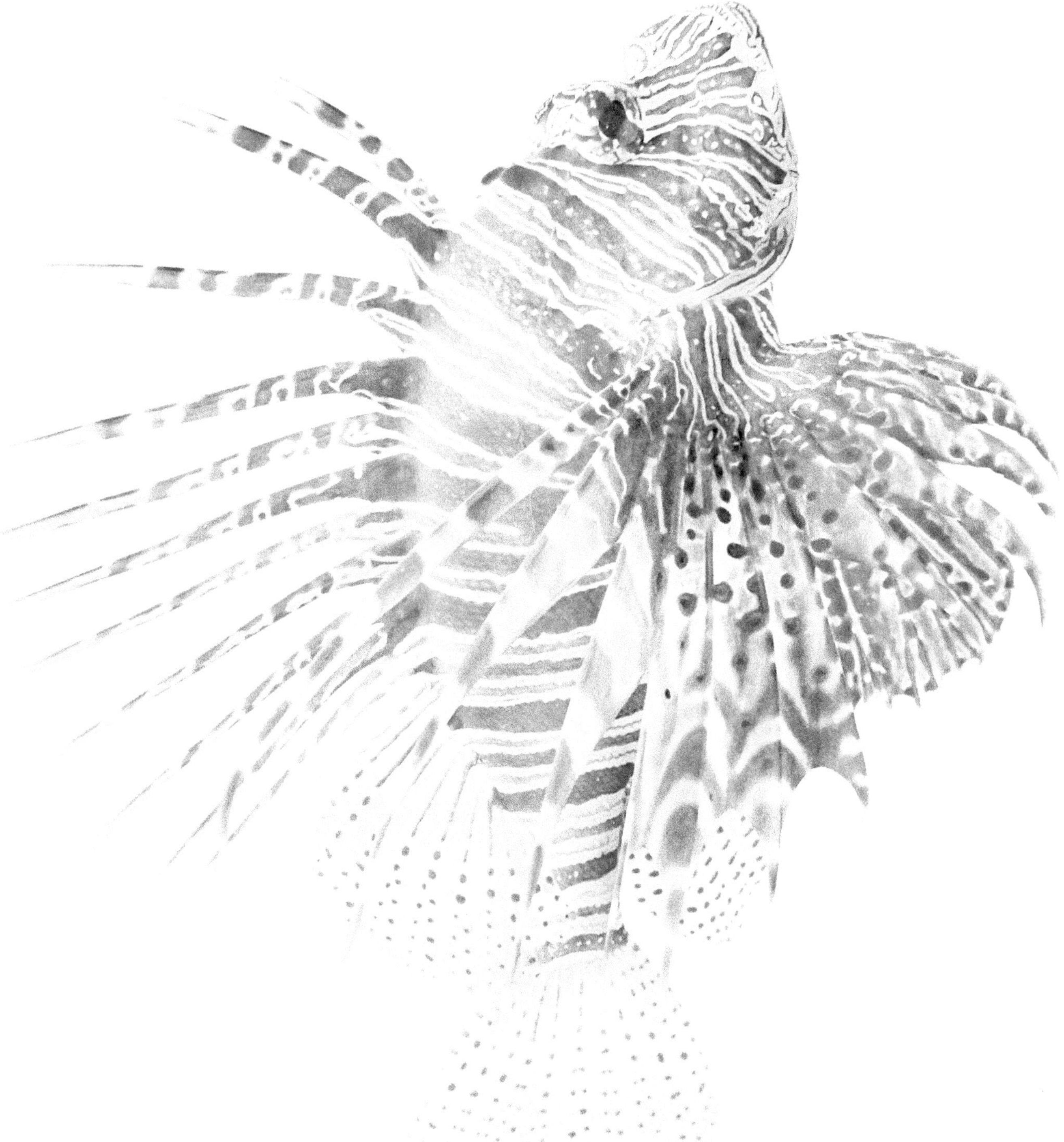

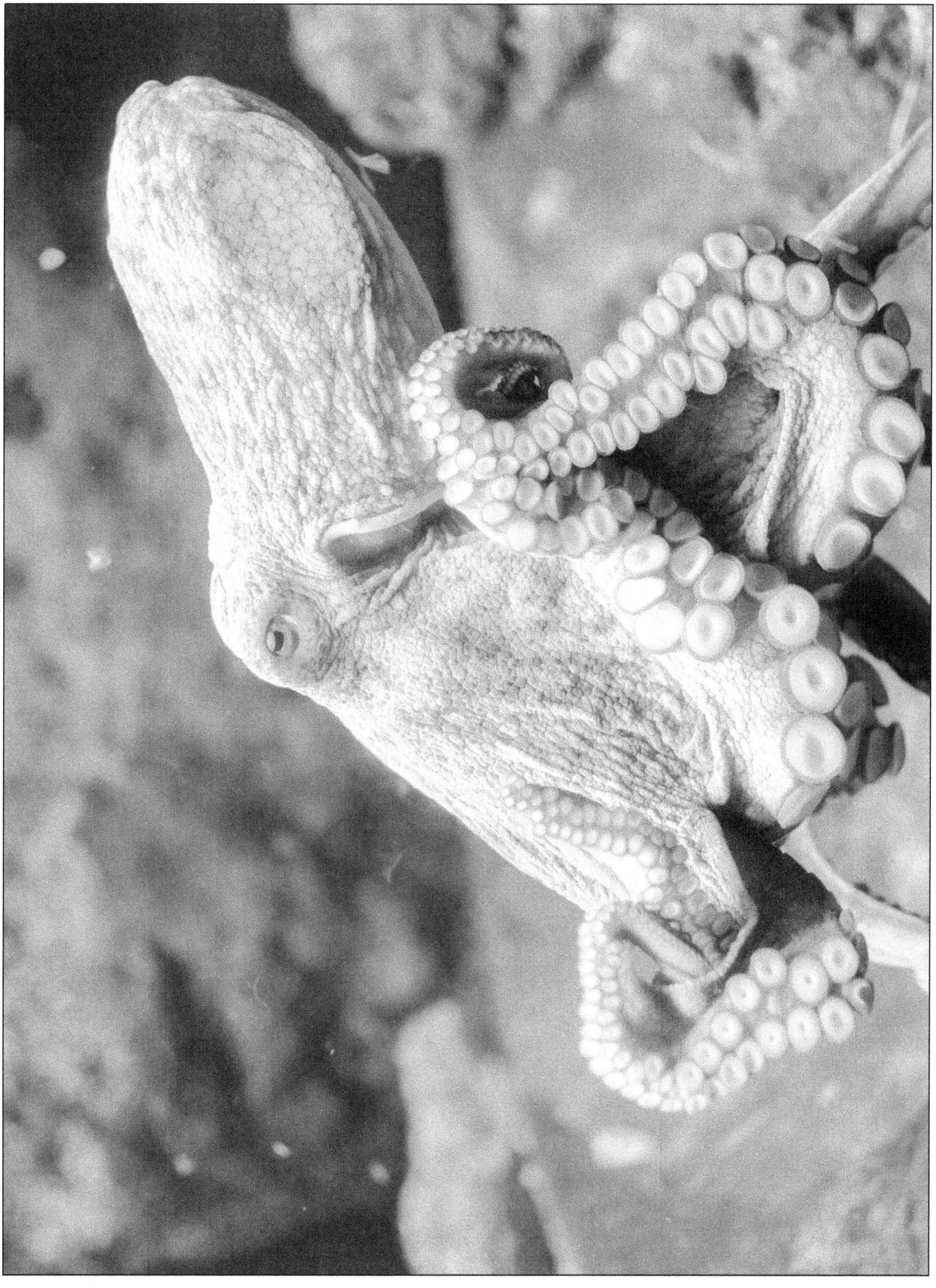

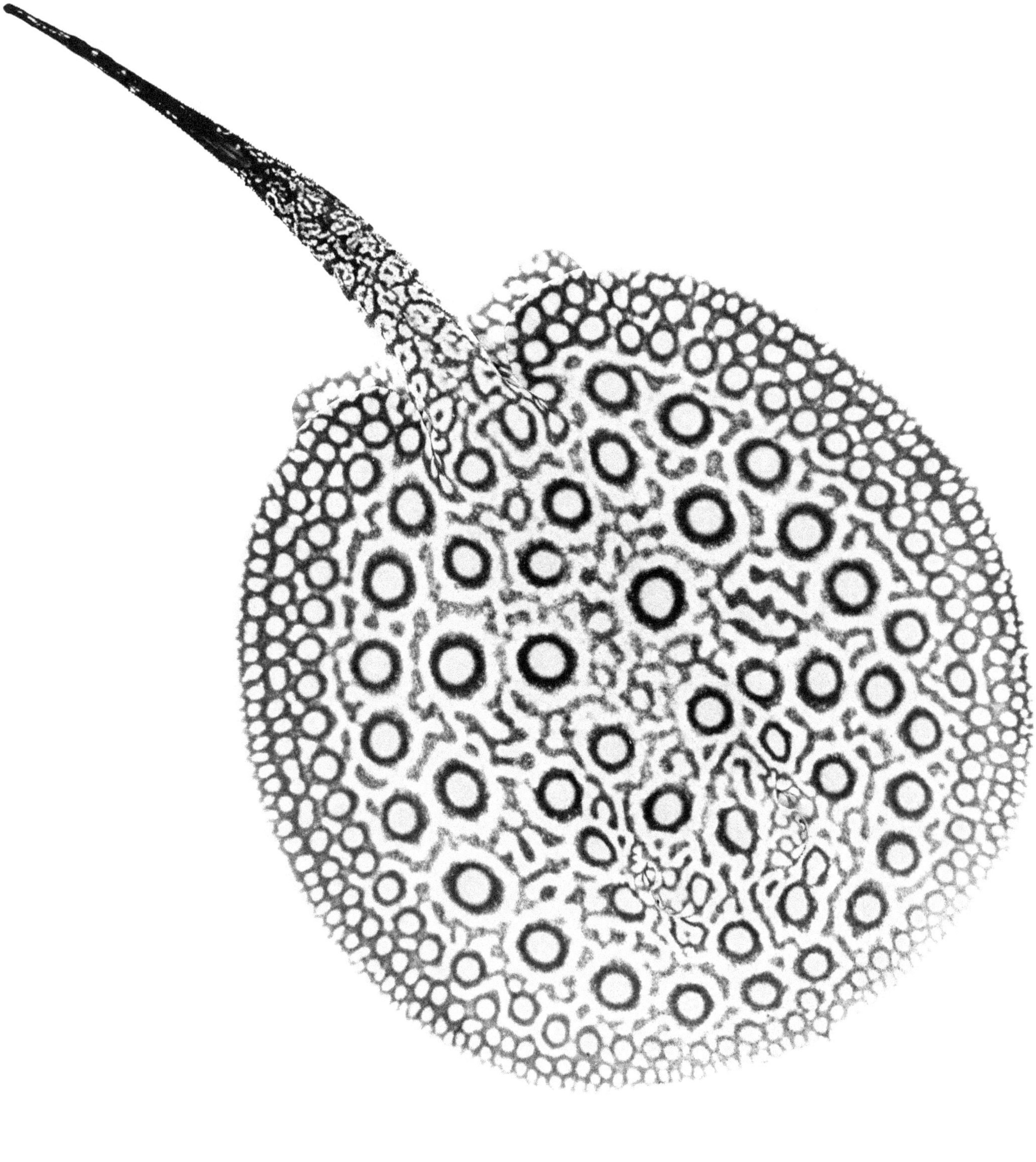

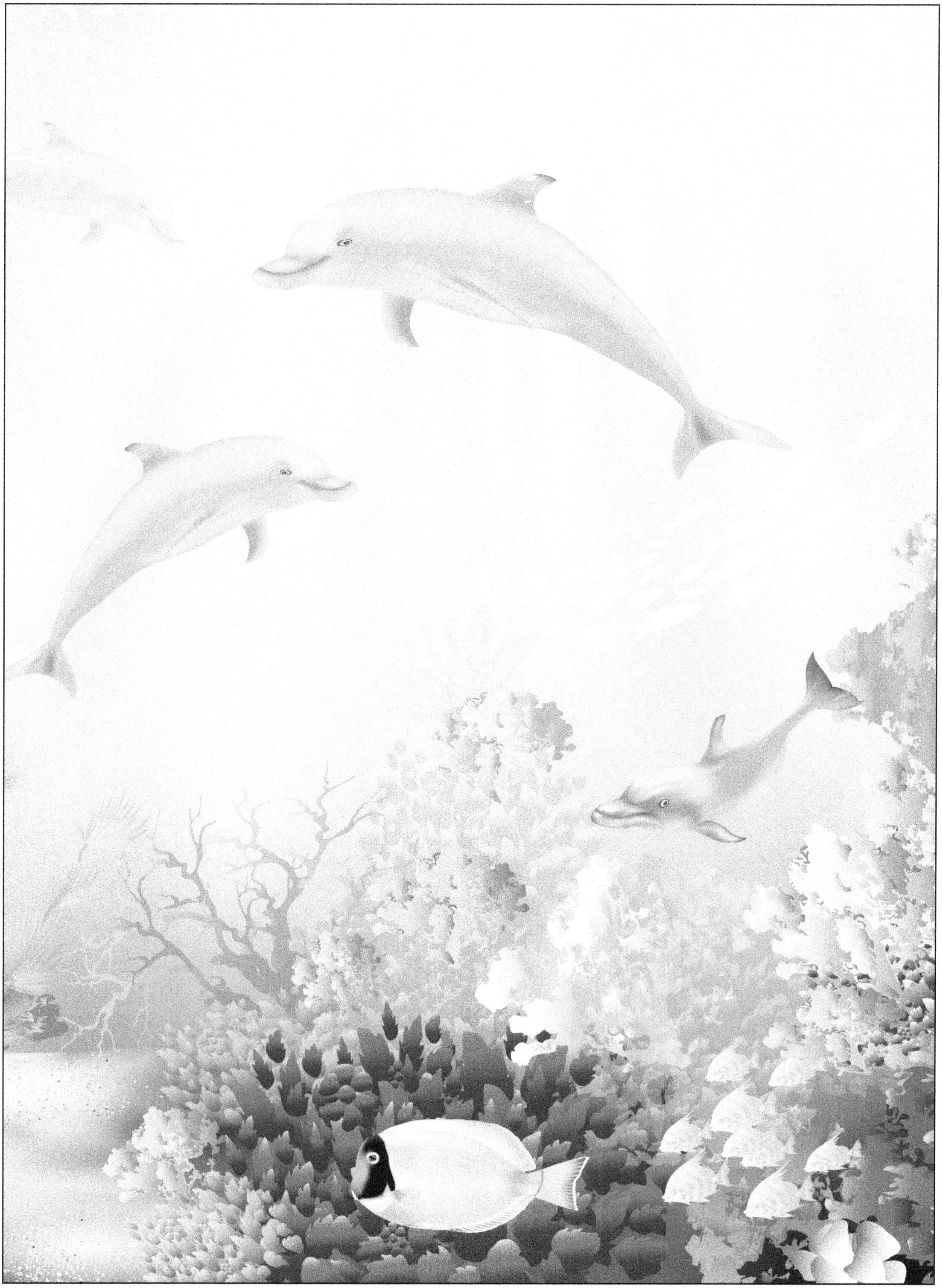

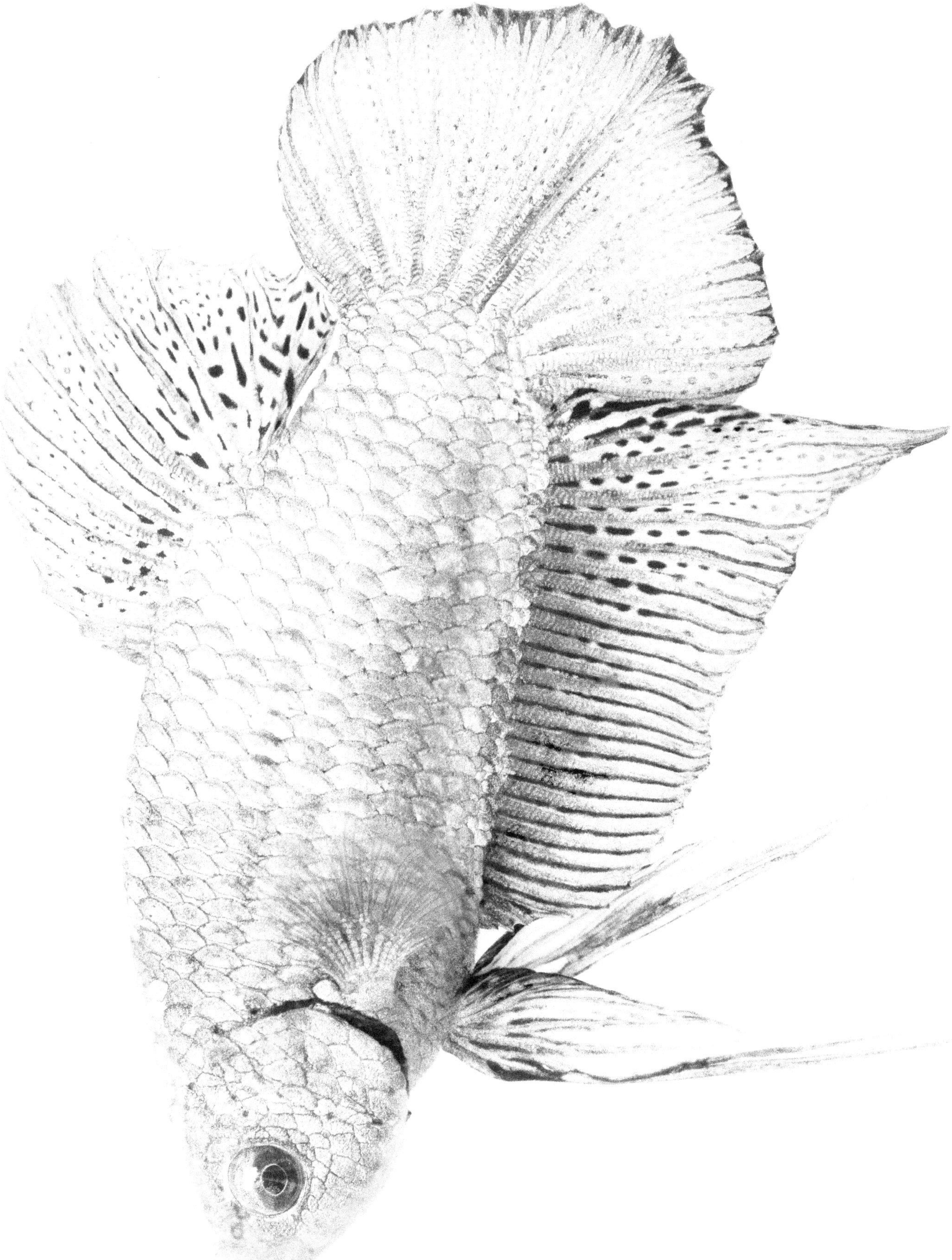

www.ingramcontent.com/pod-product-compliance
Lightning Source LLC
Chambersburg PA
CBHW080603190526
45169CB00007B/2861